Poems for Pale People:
A Volume of Verse

Edwin C. Ranck

Poems for Pale People

A Volume of Verse

By

Edwin C. Ranck

1906

PREFACE

This little volume was written for no reason on earth and with no earthly reason. It just simply happened, on the principle, I suppose that "murder will out. " Murder is a bad thing and so are nonsense rhymes. There is often a valid excuse for murder; there is none for nonsense rhymes. They seem to be a necessary evil to be classed with smallpox, chicken-pox, yellow fever and other irruptive diseases. They are also on the order of the boomerang and eventually rebound and inflict much suffering on the unlucky verse-slinger. So you see nonsense, like a little learning is a dangerous thing and should be handled with as much care as the shotgun which is never known to be loaded.

A man who writes nonsense may become in time a big gun. But this is rare; more often he becomes a small bore. This appears paradoxical and will probably require thinking over, but the more you think it over the less you will understand. This is true of parlor magic. It is also true of the magazine poets. It really never pays to think. Thinking is too much like work. After reading these rhymes you will not think that the writer ever did think, which after all is the right way to think.

When Dryden wrote "Alexander's Feast" he modestly stated that it was the grandest poem ever written. Mr. Dryden evidently believed this or he wouldn't have said so. But then every one did not agree with Mr. Dryden. Now I am going one step further and will positively state that the writer of this volume is the greatest poetical genius who has not yet died in infancy.

This is an astounding statement but it can be corroborated by admiring friends, for the writer is like a certain brand of children's food in that he is advertised by his loving friends.

Speaking of "Alexander's Feast" it simply cannot be compared to any one of the finished, poetic gems in this collection because it is so utterly different. The difference is what made Dryden famous. But comparisons are odious, and Mr. Dryden has been dead several years.

"But what, " you may ask, "is the object of nonsense verse? " Most assuredly to make one laugh. That masterpiece of nonsense "Alice In Wonderland" and its companion volume "Through The Looking Class" are absurd books, but their very absurdity is what appeals to us most. Their author, Mr. Lewis Carroll was, in private life a very sober gentleman (at

least we hope so). Nonsense is the salt of life with which we season the dry food of everyday cooking.

> "A little nonsense now and then
> Is relished by the wisest men."

Even serious old Longfellow had this feeling in his bones when he wrote the immortal lines which all of us recall from childhood:

> "There was a little girl
> And she had a little curl
> Which hung way down on her forehead;
> And when she was good,
> She was very good indeed,
> But when she was bad, she was horrid."

This is nonsense pure and simple and even the most ardent admirers of Mr. Longfellow must, when they try to make "forehead" and "horrid" rhyme, admit that it was very poor verse for the author of "Evangeline. "

Bret Harte flew off at a tangent when he wrote about "Ah Sin, The Chinaman, " a nonsense poem that gave "Bill Nye" his pseudonym. Oliver Wendell Holmes wrote "The Wonderful One-Hoss Shay. " Rudyard Kipling is often "caught with the goods on him" and Mark Twain wrote an "Ode to Stephen Dowling Botts. "

And Great Scott! I almost forgot that even such a gentle, domestic creature as the cow has been the unconscious inspiration of much nonsense and has doubtless often chewed the bitter cud of reflection in deploring her undesired popularity. First she was forced (very much against her will, no doubt) to jump over the moon to the undignified strains of "Hey Diddle, Diddle. " Then, just when beginning to breathe easily again after that astounding performance, Gelett Burgess came along and gave her more notoriety by raising the question as to whether there was such a thing as a "purple cow. " And even today in many of the rural districts there are old farmers who never heard of Burgess and his "purple cow" who will tell you solemnly that "there is a cow of a sort of purplish color. " Which goes to prove that after all nonsense is only sense plus—NON.

The poems in this collection have appeared from time to time in The Kentucky Post, The Cincinnati Post, The Cincinnati Commercial Tribune, Humanity and The Valley Magazine.

WHY THE MOLE IS BLIND.

In days gone by, when cows could fly
  And goblins rode on bears;
When fairies danced upon the green
  And giants moped in lairs,
There lived alone upon a shelf
  A tinsie, winsie little elf.

Just when the stars came out at night
  And moonbeams filled the earth with light,
Down from his perch this little elf
  Would jump and wander by himself.
He wore a pair of little wings
  Tied in their place by golden strings.

One day he took a kind of notion
  To take a trip upon the ocean.
He combed his hair and washed his face
  And put his little wings in place,
Then from his shelf he softly stole
  And went to see his friend the mole
Who gave to him a pea-green boat
  And guaranteed that it would float.

A funny thing about this boat
  'Twas patterned from a ten-pound note.
The little elf was greatly pleased
  And laughed until he sneezed and sneezed;
He launched his boat upon the sea
  And kicked his little heels in glee.

The mole looked on in glad surprise
  (For in those days all moles had eyes.)
He shouted out a loud farewell
  As the little row-boat rose and fell.
The elf picked up a golden oar
  And soon lost sight of mole and shore.

The elf rowed out for quite a way
  And in the waves did sport and play,

1

Until at length the sun sank low
  And then he thought it time to go.
Now just as luck would have it then
  A prowling sea gull left his den.

The savage sea gull loudly laughed
  To see an elf in such a craft,
And swooping down upon the water
  He did a thing he hadn't oughter,
For with his strong and sturdy beak
  He caused the boat to spring a leak.

He said he longed for a little change
  And the bank-note boat was just in range;
The poor young elf gave one big holler
  Just as the sea gull made a swallow
(And this is strange indeed to follow
  For a gull himself is just a swallow.)

The faithful mole heard this loud yell
  And rushed down to the shore pell-mell.
Alas, alas he was too late
  And saw his friend's unhappy fate;
He groaned, and shrieked and tore his fur
  And raised an awful din and stir.

The sea gull heard this awful racket
  And seized the mole, just like a packet.
He carried him across the seas
  To teach the young gulls A B C's.
But the loving mole went blind with rage
  And they had to put him in a cage,
And ever since that fatal night
  The moles have all been out of sight.

NOW THERE'S A COON IN THE MOON.

There was once an eccentric old coon,
  Who ate dynamite with a spoon,
But when he got loaded
  The powder exploded—
And now there's a coon in the moon.

THE COUNTY FAIR.

Oh, let's go out to the county fair
  And breathe the balmy country air,
And whittle a stick and look at the hosses,
  Discuss the farmer's profit and losses.

We'll take a look at the country stock
  And drink some milk from a dairy crock;
Look at the pigs and admire the chickens,
  And try to forget it's hot as the dickens.

Forget there are any political rings
  Just think of the butter and eggs and things;
So wash off the buggy and hitch up the mare,
  And we'll all go out to the county fair.

O'DOWD OF THE JEFFERSON CLUB.

A maddened horse comes down the street,
  With waving mane and flying feet.
The crowd scatters in every direction;
  It looks like a fight at a city election.
A big policeman waves his hands,
  And the air is full of vague commands,
While across the street a retail grocer
  Shrieks to his child as the horse draws closer
When suddenly out of the mad hubbub,
  Steps Jimmie O'Dowd of the Jefferson Club.

Every man there holds his breath—
  To stop the horse means sudden death.
But quick as a flash,
  O'Dowd makes a dash.
With all his might and the horse's mane,
  He brings the old plug to a halt again.
Then every man there doffs his hat
  And cries "Well, what do you think of that?"
Never since the days of Nero
  Has there been a greater hero.

HALLOWEEN.

A night when witches skim the air,
  When spooks and goblins climb the stair;
When bats rush out with muffled wings,
  And now and then the door-bell rings;
But just the funniest thing of all
  Is 'cause you can't see when they call.

SATURDAY ON THE FARM.

'Tis Saturday morn and all is bright
  By nature's own endowing;
The sun is fiercely giving light,
  And only me—
      Plowing.

Across the river I hear the sound
  Of a boatman slowly rowing;
I have no time to fool around,
  Especially when I'm—
      Hoeing.

And when the dinner hour has come,
  And thoughts of work are fleeting,
I only hear the insects hum,
  Because I'm busy—
      Eating.

At night when all things are at rest,
  Safe in Old Morpheus' keeping,
No troubles do my mind infest,
  For I am soundly—
      Sleeping.

LOVING JOHN.

John went into the garden one day
  And found his baby sister at play;

John hit baby with a brick
  And laughed because it made her sick.

John is only two and six
  And loves to do these funny tricks.

THE CIRCUS.

O, the circus parade! O, the circus parade!
  It lays all the politics back in the shade,
And the merchants forget that they've got any trade,
  While many remember they've never been paid
As they rushed out to look at the circus parade;
  And preachers who used to be terribly staid
Yell just like boys at the circus parade.
  Every one's there, both the mistress and maid,
All looking on at the circus parade.

And out at the grounds, when you've seen the parade,
  How delicious it is to drink pink lemonade;
And look at the elephant twirling his trunk,
  And laugh at the capers cut by the monk;
Watch the old clown who is acting a dunce,
  And try hard to see three rings going at once;
Gaze at the ringmaster cracking his whip,
  And watch the tight-rope artist skip.
I saw that circus, Yes Sirree!
  Saw about enough for three.

LENT.

"Oh lend me five," the young man cried,
  "My money all is spent."
The maiden shook her head and sighed,
  "I'm sorry but it's Lent."

THE PROCESSIONAL.

(Written in collaboration with R. B. Hamilton.)

When Julius Caesar met his death,
  He muttered in his dying breath:
"It is not patriotism now
  Prompts you to break your friendship's vow."
Quoth Brutus, as he stabbed again
  The greatest of his countrymen:
    "You're in this fix
    Through politics."

As on his path Columbus sped,
  A sailor to the great man said:
"Without a break, without a bend,
  The broad Atlantic has no end."
And to the sailor at his side,
  'Tis rumored, that great man replied:
    "I guess I know.
    You go below."

The snow fell fast on Russia's soil,
  The soldiers, wearied with their toil,
Cried: "'Tis not possible that we
  Our native France again shall see."
Stern ever in the face of death,
  Napoleon said beneath his breath:
    "Go take a walk,
    I hate such talk."

A cherry tree lay on the ground,
  On George's body, pa did pound;
"But pa," George cried, "It seems to me
  That you are wrong; dis ain't your tree."
The old man sadly shook his head
  And to his wayward son he said:
    "Don't lie to me
    I know my tree."

When Dewey on his flagship sailed,
  The Spaniards never even quailed.
"Oh, it ain't possible," said they,
  "For him to reach Manila Bay."
But Dewey merely smiled in glee,
  "It isn't possible?" quoth he,
    "Why, hully gee,
      Just wait and see."

MORAL.

Thus onward as through life we go,
  Amid the pomp, and glare, and show,
We oft some proverb misconstrue
  And mutter boldly, "'Tis not true."
But in their calm, majestic way,
  We hear the tongues of wise men say:
    "You go way back
    And then sit down."

AT THE TELEPHONE.

Ting-ling—"South, please, 1085;
  Why hello, Jim—Oh, Saints alive!
It's south, I told you—hello; no,
  I said once that I could not go.

"Say, can you meet me there tonight?
  Confound it, Jim, you must be tight.
What are you saying anyhow,
  I've got the wrong ear by the sow?

"Not pretty? Why, she's out o'sight,
  Oh, shut up; that will be all right.
You can't walk there? Why it ain't far;
  We get there on a 'lectric car.

"Well, Great Scott, man, don't talk all day,
  But let me know now right away.
Miss B— —, Oh, let the old girl wait;
  We won't be out so very late.

"You will? All right then—eight o'clock;
  Be sure and meet me on the block,
Remember now, don't get it wrong;
  All right, old man (Ting-ling), so long."

A HARDSHIP.

I never saw a loaf of bread
  Conspicuous in its purity,
But that I sadly shook my head
  And left five-cents as surety.

CHRISTMAS TOYS.

Say, I like toys,
  Christmas toys.
Remember when we were boys
  Long ago?
Then you were a kid
  Not a beau.
And on Christmas Day,
  Oh, say,
We got up in the dark
  And had a jolly lark
Round the fire.
  The cold air was shocking
As we peeped in our stocking—
  And, way down in the toe,
Now say this is so—
  Dad placed a dollar.
Made me holler.
  Yes, sirree,

They were good to me.
  Remember Jim?
Mean trick I did him.
  You know Jim was surly?
Well I got up early
  Took his dollar out,
And put a rock
  In his sock.
Gee, he was mad,
  Went and told dad;
But dad he just laughed
  And said:
Might's well be dead
  If you couldn't have fun.
Then for spite,
  I kept that dollar 'til night.
Funny, seein' these toys
  Made me think of us boys.
But now, Gee!
  Christmas ain't like it used to be.

THE RUBAIYAT OF A KENTUCKIAN.

Wake for the sun, that scatters into flight,
  The poker players who have stayed all night;
Drives husbands home with reeling steps, and then—
  Gives to the sleepy "cops" an awful fright.

I sometimes think that never blows so red
  The nose, as when the spirits strike the head;
That every step one takes upon the way
  Makes him wish strongly he were home in bed.

The moving finger writes, but having "pull",
  You think that you can settle things in full,
But when you interview the Police Judge,
  You find that you have made an awful bull.

Some nonsense verses underneath the bough,
  A little "booze", a time to loaf, and thou—
Beside me howling in the wilderness,
  Would be enough for one day anyhow.

THE MEDICINE MAN.

Good people if you have the mumps,
  Or ever get down with the dumps;
Or have bad cold or aching pains,
  Or ever suffer with chilblains—
Don't seek your doctor for advice,
  And pay him some tremendous price,
But buy a drug that's safe and sure—
  In fact, get Blank's Consumptive Cure.

ALAS.

He led her out across the sand,
  And by her side did sit:
He asked to hold her little hand,
  She sweetly answered, "Nit."

THE GLORIOUS FOURTH AND ITS MEMORIES.

Have you ever mused in silence upon a summer's day
  And let your thoughts run riot and your feelings have full sway,
As you sprawled full length upon the grass in some secluded dell
  And breathed the balmy country air, and smelt the country
  smell?

Then as you muse,
  And gently snooze,
Between thinks
  You remember those jinks
When spirits were high
  On the Fourth of July.

There was little Willie Browning, the worst of all the boys
  Who had a sure-nuff cannon that made all kinds of noise;
And when the cannon wouldn't go he blew into the muzzle,
  But what became of Willie's teeth has always been a puzzle.

How the folks looked askance
  At the seats of our pants,
When those giant skyrockets
  Went off in our pockets!
Gee whiz!
  What fun the Fourth is!

When the red-hot July sun began to wink the clouds away,
  We were out with whoops and shoutings to celebrate the day.
With piece of punk in one hand and crackers in the other,
  We would troop home later in the day for linseed oil and mother.

But our burns
  Were small concerns.
Our hearts were light,
  Injuries slight.
Not even a sigh
  On the Fourth of July.

And as you lie and ponder, the thought comes home to you
  That your youngest boy now celebrates the way you used to do;

And the mother that he bawls for to have those small wounds
dressed
Is the woman whom long years ago you swore you loved the
best.

But what funny things
Memory brings.
Who would have thought
That I would be caught
With a tear in my eye
On the Fourth of July.

KEEP TRYIN'.

When you're feelin' blue as ink
  An' your spirits 'gin to sink,
Don't be weak an' take a drink
  But
      Keep Tryin'.

There are times when all of us
  Get riled up and start a muss,
But there ain't no use to cuss,
  Just
      Keep Tryin'.

When things seem to go awry,
  And the sun deserts your sky,
Don't sit down somewhere and cry,
  But
      Keep Tryin'.

Everybody honors grit,
  Men who never whine a bit—
Men who tell the world, "I'm IT"
  And
      Keep Tryin'.

Get a hustle on you NOW,
  Make a great, big solemn vow
That you'll win out anyhow,
  And
      Keep Tryin'.

All the world's a battlefield
  Where the true man is revealed,
But the ones who never yield
      Keep Tryin'.

GENIUS.

There was once a young man quite erratic
  Who lived all alone in an attic,
He wrote magazine verse
  That made editors curse,
But his friends thought it fine and dramatic.

TALE OF THREE CITIES.

A seedy young man in Savanah
  Fell in love with a rich girl named Anna,
But her papa got mad
  And swore that "By Gad,
The fellow shall never Havana!"

But the couple eloped to Caracas,
  Where the Germans kicked up such a fracas;
And he said to his wife,
  "You can bet your sweet life
That papa dear never will track us."

MODERN MAUD MULLER.

Maud Muller on a summer's day,
  Raked the meadows, sweet with hay.
Nor was this just a grand-stand play;
  Maud got a rake-off, so they say.

NOCTURNE.

A cat duet.
  A silhouette.
A high brick wall,
  An awful squall.
A moonlit night,
  A mortal fight.
A man in bed,
  Sticks out his head.
Gee Whiz!
  The man has riz.
His arm draws back
  A big bootjack—
A loud swish,
  Squish!
"What's that?"
  A dead cat.

THE SISSY BOY.

Beware the Sissy Boy my child,
  Not because he's very wild;
The Sissy Boy is never that,
  Although he'll run if you say "Scat!"
The Sissy Boy's infinitesimal,
  He is not worth a duodecimal.

If you should take a custard pie
  And hit a Sissy in the eye,
He would not go before a jury,
  He'd only blush and say "Oh Fury!"
For he is perfumed, sweet and mild,
  That's just his kind, my dearest child.

One should never strike a Sissy,
  He is too lady-like and prissy.
You do not need to use your fist
  But merely slap him on the wrist,
And if this will not make him budge,
  Then glare at him and say "Oh Fudge!"

The Sissy sports a pink cravat
  And often wears a high silk hat;
His voice is like a turtle dove's
  And he always wears the "cutest" gloves.
At playing ping-pong he's inured,
  And his finger-nails are manicured.

He uses powder on his face
  And his handkerchiefs are trimmed with lace;
He loves to play progressive euchre
  And spend his papa's hard-earned lucre.
He wears an air of nonchalance
  And always takes in every dance.

Socially, he's quite a pet
  And always fashionably in debt.
He hates to be considered slow
  And poses as a famous beau.

He loves to cut a swath and dash
  When papa dear puts up the cash.

This, my child, is the Sissy Boy
  Who acts so womanly and coy.
His head's as soft as new-made butter;
  His aim in life is just to flutter;
Yet he goes along with unconcern
  And marries a woman with money to burn.

TO GELETT BURGESS.

I never saw a purple cow,
  You say you never saw one;
But this I'll tell you anyhow,
  I know that I can draw one.

THE LOBSTER.

Lobsters haven't any feet,
  But they have lots of claws;
Yet lobster meat is good to eat,
  And this is strange, because —
A dog is never good to eat,
  And yet a dog has paws,
And so have cats, and so have rats
  And so have other kind of brats.

A lobster then, so to speak,
  Is, my child, an awful freak;
For if you get him in a stew,
  He'll blush quite red and glare at you.
Yet if you eat much lobster salad,
  It will make you very pallid.

A PUN FROM THE DEEP.

A funny thing once happened to a German from Berlin,
  For once he got too gay and seized a swordfish by the fin,
This made the big fish angry, and he sawed the German's chin.
  "Just Tell Them That I Saw You" said the swordfish with a grin.

STYLISH.

There once was an old crocodile
  Who lived on the banks of the Nile.
One day, for a meal,
  He swallowed a wheel,
And ate for dessert, an automobile.

IF I COULD FLY.

(What the Little Boy Thought.)

If I had wings just like a bird
  Do you know what I'd do?
I'd fly way up into the sky
  An' holler down at you.

I'd fly along the Milky Way
  Feelin' fine and chipper,
An' then I'd drink some buttermilk
  Fresh from out the Dipper.

I'd skim along through fleecy clouds,
  An' see the great, Big Bear
An' ask him how he liked to live
  So high up in the air.

Wouldn't it be dandy
  To fly just when you please,
An' go an' ask the Dog-star
  If he worried much with fleas?

I'd do all kinds of other things
  If I could only fly,
But I am just a little boy
  An' so I dassn't try.

A HAND-ME-DOWN.

Said Sue to her suitor:
  "You'll get a new suit, or
I'll sue for a suitor to suit."
  "Why Sue," said her suitor
Who tried hard to suit her,
  "Your suitor is suited to suit."

FAREWELL SNOW.

(After Walt Whitman.)

That light, that white, that weird, uncanny substance we call snow
  Is slowly sifting through the bare branches—and ever and anon
My thoughts sift with the drifting snow, and I am full of pale
  regret.
  Yes, full of pale regret and other things—you know what I mean.
And why? Because the snow must go; the time has came to part.
  Yes, it cannot wait much longer—like the flakes my thoughts are
  melting
'Tis here, 'tis there, in fact, 'tis everywhere—the snow I mean.
  Like the thick syrup which covers buckwheat cakes it lies.

The man who says he don't regret its passing also lies.
  And wilt thou never come again? Yes, thou ilt never come again.
  Alas!
How well I remember thee! 'Twas but yesterday, methinks.
  When a great daub of snow fell from a nearby housetop
And when I ventured—poor foolish mortal that I was—to look,
  Caught me fairly in the mouth (an awful swat) and nearly
  smothered me.
There is another little trick of thine, most lovely snow—
  It is but a proof of thine affection to cling around our necks,
But still we swear—we cannot help it, Snow.
  Now it is "Skidoo," or "23 for you." Oh, cursed inconstancy of
  man!

THE SAD TURKEY GOBBLER.

O a fat turkey gobbler once sat on a limb
  And he sighed at the wind, and the wind sighed at him.
But the grief of the gobbler one could not diminish,
  For it was Thanksgiving and he saw his finish.
So the heart of the gobbler was heavy as lead
  And he muttered the words of the poet who said:
"Backward, turn backward, O Time in thy flight,
  Make me a boy again, just for to-night!"

SPRIG HAS CUB.

Sprig, Sprig—Oh lovely Sprig!
  Oh, hast thou cub to stay?
Add wilt the little birdies sig
  Throughout the livelog day?
What bessage dost thou brig to be,
  Fair Lady of by dreabs—
Dost whisper of the babblig brook
  Ad fishig poles ad streabs?

Those happy days have cub agaid,
  The sweetest of the year,
Whed bad cad raise ad appetite
  Ad wholesub thirst for beer.
I've often thought id wudder, Sprig,
  Of how the lily grows,
But the thig that's botherig be dow
  Is how to sprig dew clothes.

Sprig, Sprig—Oh lovely Sprig!
  By thoughts are all of you
I saw a robid yesterday—
  How strange it seebs—ad dew!
I've got a dreadful cold, Fair Sprig,
  Or else I'd sig to thee
Ad air frob Beddelssohd, perhaps,
  Or "The Shade of the Old Apple Tree."

THE HOT WEATHER FIEND.

Ah, somewhere in another world
  There is a warmer spot,
Where the fire is burning always.
  And always it is hot;
And always fiends are shouting,
  And always flames are blue,
And always Satan's asking:
  "IS IT HOT ENOUGH FOR YOU?"

WHEN THE LID WAS ON.

They were seated there in silence
  Each one busy with a frown,
It was midnight in the city,
  And the lid was on the town.
They had all been playing poker
  'Mid the rattle of the chink,
When a gloom fell o'er the party,
  For they couldn't buy a drink,
But a little fellow whispered
  As he held a poker hand,
"Can't we get as drunk on water
  As we can upon the land?"
Then we kicked the little rascal,
  And we spoke without a frown,
And we anchored safe in harbor
  When the lid was on the town.

THE DOODLE BUG.

Why that's a doodle bug, my child
  Who lives alone, remote and wild.
His domicile's a hole in the ground
  And when at home he's easily found.
The only plan allowed by law
  Is to lure him forth upon a straw,
For the doodle bug is a misanthrope
  And otherwise is sure to elope.

GRIT.

I hate the fellow who sits around
  And knocks the livelong day —
Who tells of the work he might have done;
  If things had come his way.
But I love the fellow who pushes ahead
  And smiles at his work or play —
You can wager when things do come around,
  They will come his way — and stay.

THE NEXT MORNING.

What a difference in the morning
  When you try to raise your head;
When your eyelids seem so heavy
  You could swear they were of lead;
When your tongue is thickly coated
  And you have an awful thirst;
When you drink so much cold water
  That you feel about to burst;
When you lift your hand towards heaven
  And solemnly do say:
"I'm going to 'cut out' drinking
  And I'll swear off right to-day."

A WONDERFUL FEAT.

I never walk along the street
  Because I haven't any feet;
Nor is this strange when I repeat
  That I am but a garden beet.

APRIL FOOL.

'Twas on the f-f-f-first of April D-D-Day,
  W-w-w-when Nature s-s-smiled and all w-w-was gay,
And I—w-w-why I was in a w-w-whirl,
  'C-c-cause I w-w-was w-w-walking w-w-with my g-g-girl.

We w-w-wandered through a leafless w-w-wood
  W-w-where many giant oak-t-t-trees s-s-stood,
And p-p-paused beside a d-d-dark g-g-green pool
  And sat d-d-down on a rustic s-s-stool.

T-t-then out I s-s-spoke in accents b-b-bold,
  And all m-m-my l-love for her I t-t-told.
She answered w-w-with a sweet, s-s-hy g-g-glance
  That pierced m-m-my h-h-heart like C-C-Cupid's l-lance.

I seized her in a t-t-tight embrace,
  And s-s-showered k-k-kisses on her f-f-face,
And t-t-told her that I'd g-g-give my l-life
  If she would only b-b-be my w-w-wife.

"Please k-k-keep your l-l-life," the m-m-maid replied
  "F-f-for I w-w-will gladly b-b-be your b-b-bride,
And y-y-you" she s-s-said, in t-t-tones quite c-c-cool,
  "W-w-why you c-c-can b-b-be my April F-F-Fool."

BRUTAL MARY.

Mary had a little lamb,
  The lamb was always buttin'
So Mary killed the little lamb
  And turned him into mutton.

YOU COULDN'T HARDLY NOTICE IT AT ALL.

There was a girl in our town
  Who dearly loved to flirt,
But the home folks never noticed it at all.
  The women in the neighborhood
All said she was too pert,
  But she never even noticed them at all.

One night a young man came to call
  Who was considered slow,
But when he got alone with her,
  He turned the lights down low.
He begged her for a little kiss,
  She softly murmured "No,"
But you couldn't hardly notice it at all.

THE ALARM CLOCK.

With a clatter and a jangle,
  And a wrangle and a screech,
How the old alarm clock wheezes
  As it sneezes out of reach!
How you groan and yawn and stretch
  In the chilly morning air,
As you pull the blankets tight,
  With your head clear out of sight—
How you swear!

A NEW VERSION.

Old Mother Hubbard
  She went to the cupboard,
To find a nice bone for her dog.
  But when she got there
The cupboard was bare,
  And now they are both on the hog.

OH SCISSORS!

I knew a young man so conceited
　That a glance at his face made you heated.
One night, playing whist,
　He was slapped on the wrist,
Because some one said that he cheated.

HE APED HER.

An impudent Barbary ape
  Once tried on a lady's new cape.
As he gave a big grin,
  The lady came in,
And—his children are still wearing crepe.

TAKE UP THE HOUSEHOLD BURDEN.

Take up the household burden,
　No iron rule of kings,
But make your family understand
　That you are running things,
Don't storm around and bluster,
　And don't get mad and swear
If in the soup is floating—
　A rag and a hank of hair.

Take up the household burden
　In patience to abide,
To curse the irate grocer
　And make your wife confide
By open speech and simple
　And hundred times made plain
How she has sought to profit
　In spending all you gain.

Take up the household burden—
　The little baby boy,
And walk the floor in anguish
　And don't let it annoy.
For when the kid seems sleepy
　And you are feeling "sold,"
There comes a cry from baby boy
　That makes your blood run cold.

Take up the household burden
　And try and be a man,
Just simply grin and bear it
　And do the best you can.
Come now and try your manhood
　And let the future go,
And listen to your elders—
　They've tried it and they know.

VITASCOPE PICTURES.

A young girl stands
  Upon the sands,
And waves her hands—
  Flirtation.

A fresh young man
  With shoes of tan,
Looks spick and span—
  Expectation.

They walk the beach,
  She seems a peach
Just out of reach—
  Vexation.

Ah what is this?
  A sound of bliss
A kiss, a kiss—
  Elation.

A father lean
  Upon the scene,
Looks awful mean—
  (Curtain.)

AN IRISH TOAST.

Here's to dear Ould Ireland,
  Here's to the Irish lass,
Here's to Dennis and Mike and Pat,
  Here's to the sparkling glass.
Here's to the Irish copper,
  He may be green all right,
But you bet he's Mickie on the spot
  Whenever it comes to a fight.
Here's to Robert Emmet, too,
  And here's to our dear Tom Moore.
Here's to the Irish shamrock,
  Here's to the land we adore.

MY LIFE AND DEATH.

(By A. Turkey Gobbler.)

I'm just a turkey gobbler,
　But I've got a word to say
And I'd like to say it quickly
　Before I pass away,
For I will get it in the neck
　Upon Thanksgiving Day.

I cannot keep from thinking
　Of poor Marie Antoinette,
She lost her head completely,
　But this is what I'll get—
They'll knock the stuffin' out o' me
　Without the least regret.

I've just a few days left now
　Before I meet my fate,
For every turkey gets the axe,
　The little and the great.
There never was a turkey born
　Who didn't fill a plate.

Only three days left now,
　Goodness, how time flies!
It brings a sadness to my heart
　And teardrops to my eyes.
Does every turkey feel that way
　Three days before he dies?

This is a very cruel world
　(I'm talking sober facts),
For I was only raised to be
　The victim of an axe—
The butt of all your silly jokes,
　And all your funny cracks.

And when you sit down Thursday
　How happy you will be,

Every person gathered there
  Will eat enough for three.
I'll be the guest of honor
  'Cause that dinner is on ME.

L'ENVOI.

I'm the ghost of that poor gobbler
  Who used to be so great,
They took my poor, neglected bones
  And piled them on a plate.
Reader, shed a kindly tear
  For my unhappy fate.

This is the common lot of all
  Upon the world's great chart;
We've got to leave a pile of bones—
  The stupid and the smart.
Even when Napoleon died
  He left a Bonaparte.

We are merely puppets
  Moving on a string,
And when we think that we are IT,
  The axe will fall—"Gezing!"
O, Grave, where is thy victory?
  O, Death, where is thy sting?

IF I WERE CITY EDITOR.

(After Ben King, Dedicated to E. Jesse Conway.)

If I were City Editor
  And you should come to my cold desk and choke,
And say, "Old man I'm actually dead broke."
  I say, if I were City Editor,
And you should come in deepest grief and woe
  And say, "Oh Lordy let me have the dough,"
I might arise with slow and solemn wink
  And lecture you upon the curse of drink.

If I were City Editor
  And you should come to my hotel and reel,
Clasping my beer to quench the thirst you feel,
  I say if I were City Editor
And you should come in trembling and in fear
  And even hint about licking up that beer,
I'd hit you just one swat, and then,
  I guess I'd have to order one more bier.

TRANSCENDENTALISM.

What is transcendentalism?
  Merely sentimentalism
With a dash of egotism
  Somewhat mixed with mysticism.
Not at all like Socialism,
  Nor a bit like Atheism,
Hinges not on pessimism,
  Treats of man's asceticism,
Quite opposes anarchism.
  Can't you name another "Ism?"
Yes, it's transcendentalism.

THE EPIC OF THE HOG.

(Man's Inhumanity to Hogs Makes Countless Thousands Squeal.)

I lived upon a little farm,
  A happy hog was I,
I never dreamed of any harm
  Nor ever thought to die.

All day I wallowed in the mud,
  And ate the choicest slops.
I watched the brindles chew their cud—
  The farmer tend his crops.

Upon the hottest days I'd go
  And flounder in the river—
I thought that hogs might come and go,
  But I would live forever.

Then finally I waxed so fat
  That I could hardly walk,
And then the farmers gather 'round
  And all began to talk.

I couldn't understand a word,
  All I did was grunt;
You see that's all a hog can do—
  It is his only stunt.

But finally they took me out
  And put me on a train.
I really couldn't move about
  And squealed with might and main.

I grunted, grunted as I flew
  And moved in vain endeavor,
But even then I thought it true
  That I would live forever.

And so we came to Packingtown
  Where there were hogs galore,

I never saw so many hogs
  In all my life before.

Then we had to shoot the chutes
  And climb a flight of stairs,
We never had a chance to stop
  Or time to say our prayers.

Loud-squealing hogs above, below
  They formed a seething river,
For men may come and men may go
  But hogs go on forever.

And then I saw an iron wheel
  Which stood alone in state,
And then I heard an awful squeal—
  A hog had met his fate.

A devilish chain upon the wheel
  Had seized him by the leg;
It was no use to kick and squeal,
  It was no use to beg.

I longed in deepest grief and woe
  To leave that brimming river;
If once into that room you go
  Your fate is sealed forever.

Farewell, Farewell, a long farewell,
  Around the room I spin,
And then a fellow with a knife
  Smites me below the chin.

  L'Envoi.

Dear reader I was just a hog,
  But O it's awful hard
To die disgraced, and then to be—
  Turned into "Pure Leaf Lard."

IN KENTUCKY.

(A Response to Judge Mulligan's Famous Toast.)

The moonlight may be softest
  In Kentucky,
And summer days come oftest
  In Kentucky,
But friendship is the strongest
  When the money lasts the longest
Or you sometimes get in wrongest
  In Kentucky.

Sunshine is the brightest
  In Kentucky,
And a right is often rightest
  In Kentucky,
While plain girls are the fewest,
  They work their eyes the truest,
They leave a fellow bluest
  In Kentucky.

All debts are treated lightest
  In Kentucky,
So make your home the brightest
  In Kentucky,
If you have the social entree
  You need never think of pay,
Or, at least, that's what they say
  In Kentucky.

Orators are the proudest
  In Kentucky,
And they always talk the loudest
  In Kentucky.
While boys may be the fliest,
  Their money is the shyest,
They carry bluffs the highest
  In Kentucky.

Pedigrees are longest

In Kentucky,
Family trees the strongest
  In Kentucky.
For blue blood is a pride,
  But, if you've ever tried
You'll find 'sporting blood' inside
  In Kentucky.

Society is exclusive
  In Kentucky,
So do not be intrusive
  In Kentucky.
If you want the right of way,
  And have the coin to pay,
You'll be in the swim to stay
  In Kentucky.

The race track's all the money
  In Kentucky,
But don't you go there, sonny
  In Kentucky.
For, while thoroughbreds are fleetest,
  They get your coin the neatest,
And leave you looking seediest
  In Kentucky.

Short-skates are the thickest
  In Kentucky,
They spot a sucker quickest
  In Kentucky.
They'll set up to a drink,
  Get your money 'fore you think,
And you get the "dinky dink"
  In Kentucky.

If you want to be fraternal
  In Kentucky,
Just call a fellow "Colonel"
  In Kentucky,
Or, give a man a nudge
  And say, "How are you, Judge?"
For they never call that "fudge"
  In Kentucky.

But when you have tough luck
  In Kentucky,
In other words "get stuck"
  In Kentucky,
Just raise your voice and holler
  And you'll always raise a dollar,
While a drink is sure to follow
  In Kentucky.

'Tis true that birds sing sweetest
  In Kentucky,
That women folk are neatest
  In Kentucky,
But there are things you shouldn't tell
  About our grand old State—and, well—
Politics is h— —l
  In Kentucky.

IN DEEPER VEIN.

The Incubus.

The way was dark within the gloomy church-yard,
  As I wandered through the woodland near the stream,
With slow and heavy tread
  Through a city of the dead,
When suddenly I heard a dreadful scream.

My heart gave frantic leap, as when the roebuck
  Is started by the clamor of the chase,
And I halted all atremble
  In the vain hope to dissemble,
Or cloak the leaden pallor on my face.

'Twas in the ghostly month of grim December,
  The frozen winds were bitter in their cry
And I muttered half aloud
  To that white and silent crowd:
"'Tis a somber month to live in or to die."

And then as if in answer to my whisper,
  Came a voice of some foul fiend from Hell:
"No longer live say I,
  'Tis better far to die
And let the falling snow-flakes sound the knell."

Perched upon a tombstone sat the creature
  Grewsome as an unquenched, burning lust.
Sitting livid there
  With an open-coffin stare—
A stare that seemed the mocking of the just.

And in my thoughts the dreadful thing is sitting—
  Sitting there with eyelids red and blear,
And see it there I will
  'Til my restless soul is still
And the earth-clods roll and rumble on my bier.

TO CLARA MORRIS.

In days gone by, the poets wrote
  Sweet verses to the ladies fair;
Described the nightingale's clear note,
  Or penned an Ode to Daphne's hair.

To dare all for a woman's smile
  Or breathe one's heart out in a rose—
Such trifles now are out of style,
  The scented manuscript must close.

Yet Villon wrote his roundelays,
  And that sweet singer Horace;
But I will sing of other days
  In praise of Clara Morris.

Youth is but the joy of life,
  Not the eternal moping;
We get no happiness from strife
  Nor yet by blindly groping.

All the world's a stage you know
  The men and women actors;
A little joy, a little woe—
  These are but human factors.

The mellow days still come and go,
  The earth is full of beauty;
If we would only think it so,
  Life is not all a duty.

And you are young in heart not years,
  Is this not true because
You mingle happiness with tears
  And do not look for flaws?

Your silver hair is but the snow
  That drifts above the roses,
And though the years may come and go
  They can but scatter posies.

REQUIESCAT.

(Mrs. Jefferson Davis, widow of the President of the Southern Confederacy died October 16, 1906.)

Oh weep fair South, and bow thy head
  For one is gone beyond recall!
Cast flowers on the sainted dead
  Who sleeps beneath a funeral pall.
  To the sound of muffled drum,
  To the sound of muffled drum.

She saw a noble husband's fame
  Grow more enduring with the years,
And in the land his honored name
  Loom brighter through a mist of tears,
  But the sound of muffled drum!
  O the sound of muffled drum!

Our fate is but to meet and part
  Upon Life's dark and troubled sea,
Yet recollection stirs the heart,
  Of men in gray who used to be,
  But the sound of muffled drum!
  O the sound of muffled drum!

Brave South, 'tis but a moment's pause
  E'er on that dim and distant shore,
The heroes of thy Fallen Cause
  Will meet again to part no more
  To the sound of muffled drum.
  To the sound of muffled drum.

CRABBED.

A college professor one day
  Was fishing in Chesapeake Bay;
Said a crab to his mate,
  "Let's kick off the bait,
This business is too old to pay."

LIFE.

The list is long, the stories read the same;
  Strong mortal man is but a flesh-hued toy;
Some have their ending in a life of shame;
  Others drink deeply from the glass of joy;
Some see the cup dashed dripping from their lip
  Or drinking, find the wine has turned to gall,
While others taste the sweets they fain would sip
  And then Death comes—the sequel to it all.

TO POE.

You lived in a land horror-haunted,
  And wrote with a pen half-divine;
You drank bitter sorrow, undaunted
  And cast precious pearls before swine.

TO A CHILD AT CHRISTMAS TIME.

May the day that gave Christ birth
  Bring you boundless joy and mirth,
Fill the golden hours with gladness,
  Raise no thought to cause you sadness.

[1]THE WAR OF THE RATS AND MICE.

Far back within an age remote,
  Which common history fails to note,
When dogs could talk, and pigs could sing,
  And frogs obeyed a wooden king,
There lived a tribe of rats so mean,
  That such a set was never seen.
For during all the livelong day
  They fought and quarrelled in the hay,
And then at night they robbed the mice,
  Who always were so kind and nice.
They stole their bread, they stole their meat,
  And all the jam they had to eat;
They gobbled up their pies and cake,
  And everything the mice could bake;
They stuffed themselves with good fresh meal,
  And ruined all they could not steal;
They slapped their long tails in the butter
  Until they made a frightful splutter;
Then, sleek and fine in coats of silk,
  They swam about in buttermilk.
They ate up everything they found,
  And flung the plates upon the ground.
And catching three mice by their tails,
  They drowned them in the water-pails;
Then seeing it was morning light,
  They scampered home with all their might.
The mouse-tribe living far and near,
  At once this awful thing did hear,
And all declared with cries of rage,
  A war against the rats they'd wage.
The mouse-king blew a trumpet blast,
  And soon the mice came thick and fast
From every place, in every manner,
  And crowded round the royal banner.
Each had a sword, a bow and arrow;
  Each felt as brave as any sparrow,
And promised, in the coming fight,
  To die or put the rats to flight.
The king put on a coat of mail,

And tied a bow-knot to his tail;
He wore a pistol by his side,
  And on a bull-frog he did ride.
"March on!" he cried. And, hot and thick,
  His army rushed, in double quick.
And hardly one short hour had waned,
  Before the ranks the rat-camp gained,
With sounding drum and screaming fife,
  Enough to raise the dead to life.
The rats, awakened by the clatter,
  Rushed out to see what was the matter,
Then down the whole mouse-army flew,
  And many thieving rats it slew.
The mice hurrahed, the rats they squealed,
  And soon the dreadful battle-field
Was blue with smoke and red with fire,
  And filled with blood and savage ire.
The rats had eaten so much jam,
  So many pies and so much ham,
And were so fat and sick and swollen
  With all the good things they had stolen
That they could neither fight nor run;
  And so the mice the battle won.
They threw up rat-fur in the air;
  They piled up rat-tails everywhere;
And slaughtered rats bestrewed the ground
  For ten or twenty miles around.
The rat-king galloped from the field
  When all the rest were forced to yield;
But though he still retained his skin,
  He nearly fainted with chagrin,
To think that in that bloody tide
  So many of his rats had died.
Fierce anger blazed within his breast;
  He would not stop to eat or rest;
But spurring up his fiery steed,
  He seized a sharp and trusty reed —
Then, wildly shouting, rushed like hail
  To cut off little mouse-king's tail.
The mouse-king's face turned red with passion
  To see a rat come in such fashion,
For he had just that minute said
  That every thieving rat was dead.

The rat was scared, and tried to run,
  And vowed that he was just in fun;
But nought could quell the mouse-king's fury —
  He cared not then for judge or jury;
And with his sharp and quivering spear,
  He pierced the rat right through the ear.
The rat fell backward in the clover,
  Kicked up his legs, and all was over.
The mice, with loud and joyful tones,
  Now gathered all the bad rats' bones,
And with them built a pyramid,
  Down which their little children slid.
And after that eventful day
  The mice in peace and joy could play,
For now no wicked rats could steal
  Their cakes and jam and pies and meal,
Nor catch them by their little tails,
  And drown them in the water-pails.

[1] Written by the author's father, the late George W. Ranck. It first appeared in St. Nicholas and is reprinted by permission of The Century Company.

THINGS WORTH WHILE.

To sit and dream in a shady nook
While the phantom clouds roll by;
To con some long-remembered book
When the pulse of youth beats high.

To thrill when the dying sunset glows
Through the heart of a mystic wood,
To drink the sweetness of some wild rose,
And to find the whole world good.

To bring unto others joy and mirth,
And keep what friends you can;
To learn that the rarest gift on earth
Is the love of your fellow man.

To hold the respect of those you know,
To scorn dishonest pelf;
To sympathize with another's woe,
And just be true to yourself.

To find that a woman's honest love
In this great world of strife
Gleams steadfast like a star, above
The dark morass of life.

To feel a baby's clinging hand,
To watch a mother's smile;
To dwell once more in fairyland —
These are the things worth while.